WITHDRAWN

WHICH WAY?
¿POR DÓNDE?

Grow a bilingual vocabulary by:

- **Looking** at pictures and words
- **Talking** about what you see
- **Touching** and naming objects
- **Using** questions to extend learning...
  Ask questions that invite children
  to share information.
  Begin your questions with words like...
  who, what, when, where and how.

Aumenta tu vocabulario bilingüe:

- **Mirando** las imágenes y las palabras
- **Hablando** de lo que ves
- **Tocando** y nombrando los objetos
- **Usando** preguntas para aumentar el aprendizaje...
  Usa preguntas que inviten a los niños a compartir
  la información.
  Empieza tus frases con el uso de estas palabras:
  ¿quién? ¿qué? ¿cuándo? ¿dónde? y ¿cómo?

These books support a series of educational games by Learning Props.
Estos libros refuerzan una serie de juegos educativos desarrollados por Learning Props.
Learning Props, L.L.C., P.O. Box 774, Racine, WI 53401-0774
1-877-776-7750   www.learningprops.com

Created by Creado por: Bev Schumacher, Learning Props, L.L.C.
Graphic Design Diseñadora gráfica: Bev Kirk
Images Fotos: Hemera Technologies Inc., Bev Kirk, Celia Roberts, Matthew 25 Ministries,
        Jane Lund, Photos.com, Liquid Library
Spanish Translation Traducción al español: Elaine St. John-Lagenaur, Myriam Sosa, Rosana Sartirana
Translation Consultant Asesor de traducción: Luis Pinto

LEARNING *PROPS*

Library of Congress Control Number 2004095848   ISBN 978-0-9741549-3-0

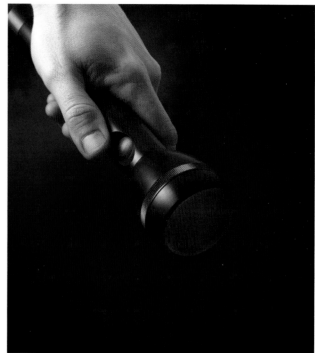

on
encender

off
apagar

in
en/dentro

out
fuera

inside
adentro

outside
afuera

open
abierto/abierta

closed
cerrado/cerrada

to open
abrir

to close
cerrar

alto

low
bajo

above
arriba

below
abajo

over
encima

under
debajo

wet
mojado/
mojada

dry
seco/
seca

© Celia Roberts

happy
feliz

sad
triste

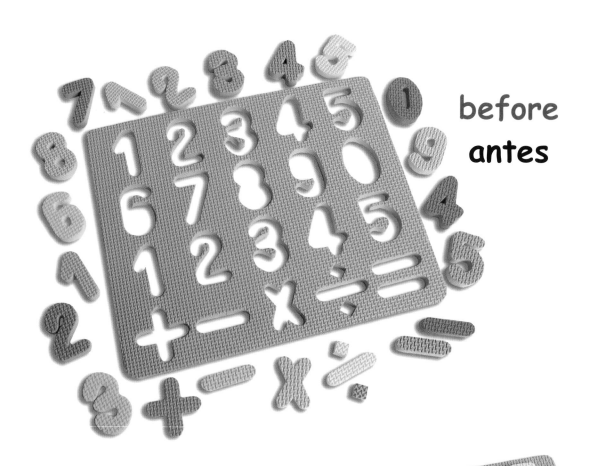

before
antes

after
después

day
el día

night
la noche

near
cerca

far
lejos

front

la parte delantera

back

la parte trasera

coming

venir

going

ir

behind
detrás

between
entre

in front
en frente

---

it is hot
hace calor

it is cold
hace frío

hot
caliente

cold
frío/fría

ahead
adelante

back
atrás

backward
hacia atrás

forward
hacia adelante

loud/noisy
ruidoso/ruidosa

quiet
silencioso/silenciosa

push
empujar

pull
tirar/jalar

empty
vacío/vacía

full
lleno/llena

heavy
pesado/
pesada

light
liviano/liviana
ligero/ligera

left
a la izquierda

right
a la derecha

straight
ahead
**seguir
derecho**

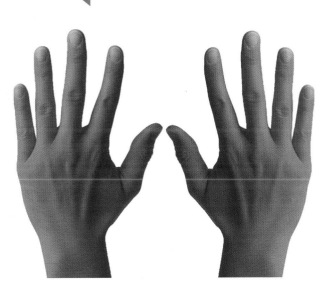

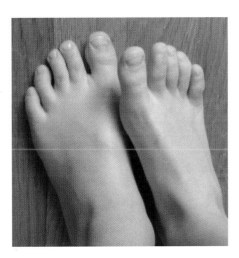

left hand
**la mano
izquierda**

right hand
**la mano
derecha**

left foot
**el pie
izquierdo**

right foot
**el pie
derecho**

big
grande

little
pequeño/pequeña

tall
alto/alta

short
bajo/baja

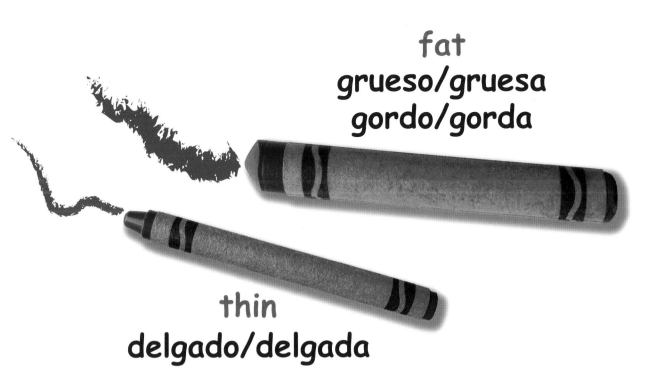

fat
grueso/gruesa
gordo/gorda

thin
delgado/delgada

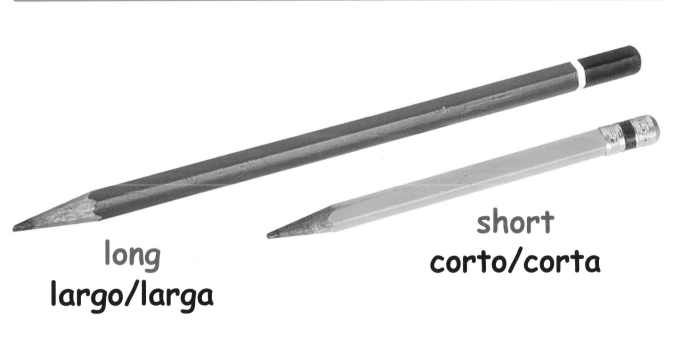

long
largo/larga

short
corto/corta

up
arriba

top
arriba

down
abajo

bottom
abajo

pronunciation
la pronunciación

on / **on**   encender / ayn-sayn-**dayr**
off / **awf**   apagar / ah-pah-**gahr**

in / **in**   en, dentro / ayn, **dayn**-troh
out / **out**   fuera / foo-**ay**-rah

inside / **in**-side   adentro / ah-**dayn**-troh
outside / **out**-side   afuera / ah-foo-**ay**-rah

open / **oh**-puhn   abierto, abierta / ah-bee-**ayr**-toh, ah-bee-**ayr**-tah
closed / **klohzd**   cerrado, cerrada / say-**rrah**-doh, say-**rrah**-dah
to open / to **oh**-puhn   abrir / ah-**breer**
to close / to **klohz**   cerrar / say-**rrahr**

high / **hye**   alto / **ahl**-toh
low / **loh**   bajo / **bah**-hoh

above / uh-**buhv**   arriba / ah-**rree**-bah
below / bi-**loh**   abajo / ah-**bah**-hoh

over / **oh**-vur   encima / ayn-**see**-mah
under / **uhn**-dur   debajo / day-**bah**-hoh

wet / **wet**   mojado, mojada / moh-**hah**-doh, moh-**hah**-dah
dry / **drye**   seco, seca / **say**-koh, **say**-kah

happy / **hap**-ee   feliz / fay-**lees**
sad / **sad**   triste / **trees**-tay

before / bi-**for**   antes / **ahn**-tays
after / **af**-tur   después / days-poo-**ays**

day / **day**   el día / ayl **dee**-ah
night / **nite**   la noche / lah **noh**-shay

near / **nihr**   cerca / **sayr**-kah
far / **far**   lejos / **lay**-hohs

front / **fruhnt**   la parte delantera / lah **pahr**-tay day-lahn-**tay**-rah
back / **bak**   la parte trasera / lah **pahr**-tay trah-**say**-rah

coming / **kuhm**-ing   venir / vay-**neer**
going / **goh**-ing   ir / eer

English	Español
behind / bi-**hinde**	detrás / day-**trahs**
between / bi-**tween**	entre / **ayn**-tray
in front / in **fruhnt**	en frente / ayn **frayn**-tay
it is hot / it iz hot (weather)	(el clima)hace calor / **ah**-say kah-**lohr**
it is cold / it iz kohld (weather)	(el clima)hace frío / **ah**-say **free**-oh
hot / **hot** (temperature)	(la temperatura) caliente / kah-lee-**ayn**-tay
cold / **kohld** (temperature)	(la temperatura) frío, fría / **free**-oh, **free**-ah
ahead / uh-**hed**	adelante / ah-day-**lahn**-tay
back / **bak**	atrás / ah-**trahs**
backward / **bak**-wurd	hacia atrás / **ah**-see-ah ah-**trahs**
forward / **for**-wurd	hacia adelante / **ah**-see-ah ah-day-**lahn**-tay

loud, noisy / **loud, noi-zee**	ruidoso, ruidosa / rroo-ee-**doh**-soh, rroo-ee-**doh**-sah
quiet / **kwye**-uht	silencioso, silenciosa / see-layn-see-**oh**-soh, see-layn-see-**oh**-sah
push / **push**	empujar / aym-poo-**hahr**
pull / **pul**	tirar, jalar / tee-**rahr**, hah-**lahr**
empty / **emp**-tee	vacío, vacía / vah-**see**-oh, vah-**see**-ah
full / **ful**	lleno, llena / **yay**-noh, **yay**-nah
heavy / **hev**-ee	pesado, pesada / pay-**sah**-doh, pay-**sah**-dah
light / **lite**	liviano, liviana; ligero, ligera / lee-vee-**ah**-noh, lee-vee-**ah**-nah; lee-**hay**-roh, lee-**hay**-rah
left / **left** (direction)	(orientación) a la izquierda / ah lah ees-kee-**ayr**-dah
right / **rite** (direction)	(orientación) a la derecha / ah lah day-**ray**-shah
straight ahead / **strayt** uh-**hed**	seguir derecho / say-**geer** day-**ray**-shoh
left / **left** (description)	(descripción) izquierdo, izquierda / ees-kee-**ayr**-doh, ees-kee-**ayr**-da
right / **rite** (description)	(descripción) derecho, derecha / day-**ray**-shoh, day-**ray**-shah
big / **big**	grande / **grahn**-day
little / **lit**-uhl	pequeño, pequeña / pay-**kay**-nyoh, pay-**kay**-nyah
tall / **tawl**	alto, alta / **ahl**-toh, **ahl**-tah
short / **short**	bajo, baja / **bah**-hoh, **bah**-hah
fat / **fat**	grueso, gruesa/groo-**ay**-soh, groo-**ay**-sah gordo, gorda / **gohr**-doh, **gohr**-dah
thin / **thin**	delgado, delgada / dayl-**gah**-doh, dayl-**gah**-dah
long / **lawng**	largo, larga / **lahr**-goh, **lahr**-gah
short / **short**	corto, corta / **kohr**-toh, **khor**-tah
up / **uhp**	arriba / ah-**rree**-bah
down / **doun**	abajo / ah-**bah**-hoh
top / **top**	arriba / ah-**rree**-bah
bottom / **bot**-uhm	abajo / ah-**bah**-hoh